The History of Rowntrees in Old Photographs

Joe Murphy

Joe Murphy
14 Church Road
York
North Yorkshire
YO10 3NW

© Joe Murphy 2007

First published December 2007

ISBN 978-0-9558012-0-4

Cover design by Clare Brayshaw

Prepared by:

York Publishing Services Ltd
64 Hallfield Road
Layerthorpe
York YO31 7ZQ
Tel: 01904 431213

Website: www.yps-publishing.co.uk

Acknowledgements

I am indebted to the following people and organisations for their generous help in the preparation of this book.

A big thank you to Melvin Browne, Mick Herd and Joe Dickenson for allowing me access to their postcard collections, especially Joe who imparted with his vast knowledge of the cocoa works.

A special thank you to Janet McCulloch librarian at the Joseph Rowntree Trust at Water End Clifton, York for her unstinting help in allowing me access to Cocoa Workers magazines, photographs, and printed ephemera.

A special mention must go to Cathy Nock, Barbara Steptoe and Kelvyn Passmore at the Joseph Rowntree Library at The Cocoa Works for their help and information on books that helped me in my quest.

A Brief Chronological History of Rowntrees

Rowntree and Company Limited

1725 A Quaker, Mary Tuke, opened grocer's shop in Walmgate, York.

1785 The firm, which had become Wm. Tuke and Sons dealt in cocoa.

1815 Wm. Tuke and Sons described themselves as tea dealers and added that they roasted coffee and made chocolate.

1859 Maximum total weekly output of cocoa was 12 cwt.

1862 Henry Isaac Rowntree acquired cocoa and chocolate side of the business.

1864 York foundry purchased and converted into cocoa and chocolate making plant.

1869 H.I. Rowntree's brother, Joseph, became partner. H.I. Rowntree and Co set up.

1879 Manufacture of pastilles and gums, then a French monopoly, began. A Frenchman, M. Gaget took charge of new department.

About 100 employees.

1881 Rowntree's Fruit Pastilles introduced.

1882 Purchase and conversion of York flour mill.

Two types of cocoa made: Rock cocoa – fine cocoa mixed with sugar and sold in blocks; and loose cocoa powder mixed with arrowroot or sago. Chocolate drops, chocolate beans and penny and halfpenny chocolate bells also made.

1883 H.I. Rowntree died, leaving Joseph in sole control.

1889	Joseph's son, Benjamin Seebohm Rowntree, entered the business.
1890	23 acres of land bought on outskirts of York where present factory stands – 'Haxby Road site'.
1893	Rowntree's Fruit Gums introduced.
1897	Limited liability company, Rowntree and Co Ltd, set up with Joseph Rowntree as Chairman, issued capital of £226,200 and about 1,200 employees.
1899	31 acres bought north of Haxby Road site.
1901	Rowntree's Table jellies introduced.
1902	House journal, 'Cocoa Works Magazine', introduced.
1904	Works doctor and dentist appointed.
1905	53 acres bought north-east of Haxby Road site.
1906	Move to Haxby Road site completed.
	Pension Scheme inaugurated.
1908	21 acres bought east of Haxby Road site.
1909	Yearsley swimming baths presented to York City.
	Employees 4,000.
1913	School rooms and gymnasium on factory site opened.
	Dining facilities for 3,000 completed.
	Suggestion Scheme inaugurated.
1914	23 acres bought east of Haxby Road site.
1916	Widows' Benefit Fund set up – one of first in UK.
1918	Inception of annual week's holiday with full pay.
	Issued capital £1m.
1919	Central Works Council established.
1920	Invalidity Fund established.
	Issued capital £2.5m.
1921	Unemployment scheme began.
	Rowntree Park presented to York City.

1923 B. Seebohm Rowntree succeeded father as Chairman.

   Profit sharing scheme inaugurated.

   Rowntree's Table jellies relaunched.

1924 Gray Dunn and Co Ltd joined the Company.

   Employees 7,000.

1925 Wilson-Rowntree (Pty) Ltd, South Africa, established.

   Joseph Rowntree died.

1926 Rowntree Mackintosh (Ireland) Limited incorporated.

1927 Rowntree Mackintosh (Australia) Pty Ltd incorporated.

   Rowntree Co Ltd, Canada, incorporated.

   W. and M. Duncan joined Company.

1928 Joseph Rowntree memorial Library opened, with about 10,000 books.

1933 Black Magic chocolates introduced.

1935 Joseph Rowntree Theatre built.

   Kit Kat (then Chocolate Crisp) and Aero introduced.

1936 New cream and employment blocks completed.

   Dairy Box introduced.

1937 Smarties introduced.

   Issued capital £3,015,000.

   First London Stock Exchange quotation.

1941 George Harris became Chairman.

1947 'Dunollie', Company's rest house, opened.

1948 Polo Mints introduced.

1952 William Wallace became Chairman.

1953 N.M.U Transport Ltd joined Company.

   Issued capital £4,015,000.

1954 Seebohm Rowntree died.

   Milk Crumb production began at Egremont factory.

1957 Lloyd Owen became Chairman.

Issued capital £5,059,349.

1958 Factory build on 'green field' site in Fawdon, Newcastle.

1961 First computer installed at York.

1962 After Eight range introduced.

1963 Valley Transport Co Ltd joined the company.

Issued capital £8,684,349.

1964 Majority shareholding in Stockmann – Rowntree and Co GmbH, Hamburg (1971 renamed Rowntree Mackintosh GmbH).

1965 Rowntree (Belgium) NV, Rowntree (Holland) NV, and Rowntree (Italy) SpA, formed (1970 renamed respectively Rowntree Mackintosh NV, NV and SpA).

Jellytots introduced.

York employees 8,760.

1966 Donald Barron became Chairman.

Creamola Food Products Ltd joined Company.

1967 Maconochie Brothers (Hadfield) Ltd and Sun-Pat Products Ltd joined Company.

1968 Stewart Esplan and Greenhough Ltd became wholly-owned member of Company.

Matchmakers introduced.

Rowntree Mackintosh Limited

1969 Merger of Rowntree and Co Ltd with John Mackintosh and Sons Ltd. Name was changed to Rowntree Mackintosh Ltd.

Agreement for Hershey Foods Corporation to market and eventually manufacture selected Group products in USA.

Girls' Continuation School closed.

Employees 28,800.

Issued capital £11,684,349.

Group turnover £112,912,000 – UK £78m; EEC (the six) £9m; Overseas £26m; Exports from UK £8m.

1970   Castleford factory opened by Duchess of Kent.

New factory completed at Leicester for Fox products.

New office block, with computer centre, completed at Haxby Road, York.

Group exports distributed to over 120 countries.

Group turnover £120,357,000 – UK £80m; EEC (the six) £11m; Overseas £29m; Exports from UK £9m.

1971   Chocolate confectionery business of Chocolat-Menier SA, Paris, joined Group.

James Stedman Ltd, Australia, acquired (1972 renamed Rowntree Hoadley Ltd).

Group newspaper, 'Rowntree Mackintosh News', replaced CWM at York and MC at Norwich – circulation 26,000.

28,000 employees and 22 factories in Group.

Ordinary share nominal value halved, and for one capitalisation issue – new capital £18m.

1972   Group received Queen's Award to Industry for Export Achievement.

Chairman received Knighthood – Sir Donald Barron.

Agreement for Fujiya Confectionery Co Ltd, Tokyo, to manufacture under licence selected Group Products for Japanese Market.

Yorkshire Moulds Ltd acquired.

Issue capital £20,684,349.

Group turnover £169,718,000 – UK £101m; EEC (the six) £25m; Overseas £43m; Exports from UK £12m.

1973   Chocolat Ibled SA joined Group.

Group turnover £204,779,000 – UK £117m; EEX (excluding UK) £37m; Overseas £1m; Exports from UK £14m.

1974   Employees: UK 22,100; Overseas 8,900.

Group turnover £252,112,000 – UK £139m; EEX (excluding UK) £52m; Overseas £61m; Exports from UK £19m.

1975 Rowntree Pension Fund and Profit Sharing Scheme extended to all UK employees.

Group turnover £316,568,000 – UK £174m; EEC (excluding UK) £66m; Overseas £77m; Exports from UK £23m.

1976 Yorkie launched.

Employees: UK 21,000; Overseas 9,000.

Rights issue to raise £12.4m – one share for every five.

Group turnover £384,921,000 – UK £198m; EEC (excluding UK) £85m; Overseas £102m; Exports from UK £31m.

1977 Majority shareholding in Chocolaterie Lanvin SA, Dijon.

Chocolat-Menier SA and Chocolat Ibled SA merged to become Rowntree Mackintosh SA.

Employees Share Option Scheme introduced – UK and France.

Capital and reserves at £124m, top £100m for first time.

Group turnover £469,212,000 – UK £249m; EEC (excluding UK) £107m; Overseas £113m; Exports from UK £50m.

1978 Group received Queen's Award for Export Achievement for the second time.

Educational Trust Fund established.

Employees' Share Option Scheme extended to Australia, Canada, Germany, Belgium, Holland and Italy.

Rights issue to raise £36.1m – one ordinary share for every four.

Sterling foreign currency bond (Eurobond) for £18m issued.

Issued capital £29,687,000.

Group turnover £562,705,000 – UK £299m; EEC (excluding UK) £140m; Overseas £124m; Exports from UK £61m.

1979 Employees' Share Option Scheme extended to Ireland.

Capitalisation issue – one ordinary share issued for every ordinary share held.

Site of Group headquarters in York occupied 149 acres – factory and car parks, 71 acres; agricultural land, 55 acres; sports fields, 23 acres.

Nuts Chocoladefabriek BV, Holland acquired.

Group turnover £601,321,000 – UK £327m; EEC (excluding UK) £148m; Overseas £126m; Exports from UK £63m.

1980   Rowntree Mackintosh (Sun-Pat) Ltd set up at Hadfield.

Drifter introduced.

Group turnover £629.8 – UK £346m; EEC (excluding UK) £142m; Overseas £142m; Exports from UK £66m.

1981   Queen's Award for Export Achievement for the third time.

Mr Kenneth Dixon became Chairman on retirement of Sir Donald Barron.

Rights issue, £42m – One ordinary share for every four.

Group turnover £688,000,000 – UK £351m (including 56.1m Exports from UK); EEC (excluding UK) £177m; Overseas £160m.

Rowntree Mackintosh plc

1982   Company name – RM Ltd changed to Rowntree Mackintosh plc.

RPC Snack Foods business acquired.

Aero Countline launched.

Group turnover £770,500,000 – UK £388m (including 62.7m exports from UK); EEC £202m; Overseas £181m.

1983   Holgates Honey Farm acquired.

Laura Second (Canada) and DeMet's (USA) acquired; Tom's Foods (USA) acquired.

Commencement of £7m computerised warehouse construction at York.

Bros brand name and manufacturing plant acquired by Group's Dutch subsidiary.

Portable Order Entry Terminals made available to UK sales representatives.

Mirage (Aero Countline) launched in Canada.

Group turnover £952m – UK £444m; Europe (excluding UK) £198m; Overseas £310m; Exports from UK £66.9m.

1984 Employees Share Option Scheme extended to South Africa and, in a limited form, to the United States.

Sterling Bonds (Eurobond) for £30m and Warrants convertible to Ordinary Shares issued.

Group Structure reorganised into 4 regions comprising United Kingdom and the Republic of Ireland, North America, Europe and International covering the rest of the world.

Group turnover £1,157m – UK £470m; Europe (excluding UK) £227m; Overseas £459m; Exports from UK £71.1m.

1985 The Original Cookie Company (USA) acquired and first Original Cookie Shop in the UK opened at Peterborough.

Anglo Bellamy, Gainsborough Craftsmen and Yorkshire Moulds businesses transferred outside the Group.

£7m automated warehouse opened in York.

Laura Secord opened 5 shops in USA.

Group turnover £1,205m – UK £488m; Europe (excluding UK) £238m; North America £344m; Australasia £52m; Rest of World £83m.

1986 Seven businesses acquired – Hot Sam (USA), de Neuville (France), Judges Honey (UK), Sunmark (USA), Norgen Vaaz (Australia), Gales (UK) and Gorant Candies (USA).

Multisnack Ltd, established in UK selling food vending products.

Franchise for Godiva chocolates awarded in UK to Elect Chocolates, a newly created UK subsidiary, and in Canada to Laura Secord.

First UK shop selling Godiva chocolates opened in London in November.

Rowntree Mackintosh (Ireland) production changed to lines for the domestic Eire market only.

New £16.75 million Kit Kat factory opened in York by HRH The Duchess of Kent.

Novo and Savana launched. Eclipse launched in UK.

Group turnover £1,290m – UK £512m; Europe (excluding UK) £285m; North America £361m; Australasia £54m; Rest of World £78m.

1987 Four new UK trading subsidiaries were incorporated – Rowntree Mackintosh Confectionery Ltd, Rowntree Mackintosh Distribution, Rowntree Mackintosh Export Ltd, Rowntree Mackintosh European Exports Ltd.

Novo distributed throughout the UK.

Kit Kat celebrated its 50th anniversary.

The company announced that it would seek shareholders approval to change the name of the holding company to Rowntree plc from 30 June 1987. At the Annual general Meeting on 28 April approval was given to the change.

Rowntree plc

New Company logo introduced to coincide with the change of holding company name.

Plans announced for a 'Chocolate Experience' Visitor Centre based at Leatham's Mill, York at a cost of £0.5m

The Company announced its intention to relocate Rowntree plc headquarters to a new office complex based at The Homestead at a cost of £4.5m.

Candice-Martial acquired.

Sooner Foods Ltd changed its name to Rowntree Snack Foods Ltd with effect from 1 October 1987.

Rowntree Mackintosh Sun-Pat Ltd changed its name to Rowntree Sun-Pat Ltd with effect from 1 October 1987.

Rowntree plc acquired Restaurants International Ltd and Richoux (Counties) Ltd.

1988   Then, in April 1988, in a dawn stock market raid, the Swiss-German Chocolate and Coffee Manufacturers Jacob Suchard unexpectedly secured a 15 per cent holding. The Rowntree Trusts, which had been decisive in their rejection of the general food bid some twenty years before, had reduced their stake in the company to a combined total of 7 per cent. Jacob Suchard had a rival in the Swiss food giant Nestlé. The British government had dismissed intervention on the ground of public interest.

Nestlés financial resources secured its victory:

Before Suchard's dawn raid, Rowntrees shares had been traded at £4.68; Nestlé paid £10.75 for its final bid, which, on the basis of 1987 profits amounted to a price-earnings multiple of more than 26.

The prize was the control of the company's powerful brands, and their potential for profitable expansion into world markets. Indeed, Rowntrees development had chiefly been a history of brands, and the price Nestlé paid for them was recognition of a fifty-year-old tradition.

Joseph Rowntree was born on May 14th 1836, in the reign of William the Fourth. His father owned a grocers shop in The Pavement in the centre of York, and the family lived above the shop.

Ann Vernon, in her book 'A Quaker Business Man', printed by William Sessions of York, sets the scene perfectly in the following paragraphs.

As she lay in her bed after her confinement, Joseph's mother listened to the noise of market day crowds outside her window, and the clamour of geese being walked in from the countryside, and the ring of solid wheels on cobblestones; and in the early hour of the morning she heard the coachman's horn announcing the departure of the 'High Flyer' of the 'Wellington' for London.

Three years before Joseph was born, Cobbett said, England's manufacturing supremacy depends upon the toil of thirty thousand little girls. England was called the workshop of the world, but when Joseph was a child about two thirds of the population still lived and worked in the country. The manufacturing towns were only dark blots on an agricultural landscape, and no one bothered much about what went on in them.

Joseph's father, also called Joseph, was the sixth son of yet another Joseph. As there had been no place for him in his father's grocery business in Scarborough, on his twenty-first birthday he came to York, riding on the outside of the coach. A friend called James Backhouse went with him to an auction which was held in the 'Elephant and Castle' in Skeldergate.

The auctioneer was unfortunately drunk, but at James Backhouse's suggestion, the two young men buried his head in a bucket of water and managed to sober him up enough to conduct his business. 28 The Pavement became the elder Joseph's property.

James Backhouse was one of two Quaker brothers who had a market garden in Toft Green. Their business outgrew their premises and they were only too happy to accept £5,700 from George Hudson so that he could build his station inside the city walls.

In 1832 the elder Joseph married Sarah Stephenson who came from Manchester. After 4 weeks honeymoon in the Lake District, he brought his bride back to The Pavement and the responsibilities of a household which now comprised a dozen people. Sarah Rowntree was only 24 at the time of her marriage, but she seemed to be undaunted by the size of her 'family'. She mothered the young apprentices, organized the difficult staggered meals made necessary by the demands of the shop, helped her husband with his accounts, and entertained a great many visitors.

In 1834 the Rowntree's first child was born, a boy called John Stephenson. Joseph was born two years later and a third boy, Henry Isaac followed in 1838. Two more children were born during this time, Hannah in 1840 and Sarah Jane in 1843.

There is also an unbroken connection between Rowntree and Company and a little grocers shop opened in Walmgate in 1725.

Mary Tuke was a Quaker, the daughter of blacksmith William Tuke II who married Sarah Merrey in 1687 (D1691), daughter of Walter Merrey, Quartermaster in Oliver Cromwell's Army. His second wife, Rebecka Smith of Thirsk, whom he married in 1693, was Mary's mother.

Mary was orphaned when young. At thirty she was a girl of courage and character and decided to go into business, struggling for five years with the Merchant Adventurers Company. The struggle was fought with obstinancy on one side and a certain amount of chivalry on the other.

But somehow they never managed to make her shut up shop. Perhaps they were only concerned to preserve some semblance of their own dignity and were too genuinely kind hearted to drive an enterprising woman out of business. The little grocers shop remained open even when Mary married Henry Frankland, a stuff weaver. She did not abandon her own trade.

In fact, soon after their marriage, her husband left his job and joined her in the shop. He in turn came into collision with the Merchant Adventurers, but there was now some money available and everything was much easier. In due course he paid his admission fee and was given the Freedom of the Fellowship, thus becoming a member of the company. Mary was left a childless widow at the age of 44. She took on her nephew, William Tuke, as an apprentice and when she died in 1752, left him all her property. William Tuke was only twenty at the time, but after some hesitation he decided to carry on in the shop himself. It had been moved from Walmgate to Coppergate in Mary's lifetime and there it remained until young Henry Isaac Rowntree joined the firm over a hundred years later.

In those hundred years, after a lean beginning, the Tukes had prospered. William Tuke lived to be 90, the grocers shop became a more specialised affair and presently chocolate and cocoa manufacturers. For three generations the management of Tuke Company descended from father to son, but in 1857 when Samuel Tuke died, neither of his sons returned to York to take over the shop at the corner of Castlegate and Coppergate.

Henry Isaac Rowntree went to work for the Tukes in 1860 after he had finished his apprenticeship in his father's shop. He had not been made a partner in the grocery business as his two elder brothers had been on their twenty-first birthdays, so it is easy to assume that his patrimony was given to him in some other form. Perhaps the elder Joseph bought his youngest son some kind of financial interest in the firm to which he moved.

Certainly in 1862, three years after the elder Joseph's death, Henry Isaac was in a position to buy the cocoa and chocolate-making department of Tuke and Company.

Henry Isaac bought an old foundry, several cottages and a public house down by the river in Tanners Moat. It was by this name that Henry Isaac's factory came to be known after he moved it from the original premises in Castlegate. It was hardly a factory at all; it employed no more than a dozen men and its output was about twelve hundred weight of cocoa a week. As time went on, Henry Isaac had a hard struggle to keep the business going and by 1869, seven years after he bought the business from Tuke and Co, he found himself in a position of some difficulty.

It was at this point that Joseph joined his younger brother, taking his capital out of The Pavement shop and putting it into the business at Tanners Moat. The Rowntrees were bred in the old tradition of family responsibility, and it was sufficiently compelling to cause Joseph to learn a new trade at thirty three years of age. Joseph took over the accounts side of the business, leaving Henry Isaac to deal with the actual manufacture of cocoa.

When the staff of twelve rose to thirty, there was little distinction between the 'Office' and the 'Factory' staff, but the chief thing required of everyone was that they should be able-bodied.

When there was need for it, the 'Office staff' had to help to carry sacks of cocoa and sugar.

'What can you do?' Joseph would ask the applicant for a job. 'Can you carry a ten stone sack of flour?' If the answer was yes the next question was usually, 'When can you start?'

The system of payment was very simple. Each employee kept his own time. At the end of the week the general foreman, a man called Hanks, went round with a hat full of silver and copper coins asking everyone in turn 'How much time has thee got?' Sometimes, if the cash did not balance against his own account, he was obliged to go around again enquiring, 'What did I give thee?' It was all very friendly and uncomplicated.

In spite of reorganisation and hard work, Rowntrees fortune was not secured in the 1870s. Sales of £7,384 in 1870 did rise to £30,890 by 1879 but profitability remained precarious and losses were made in 1873 and 1876. Only four of the firm's nineteen cocoas in 1878 made a profit although they did also account for 70 per cent of sales.

In 1879 a French confectioner named A. Claude Gaget called upon Joseph and Henry Isaac with samples of pastilles. Gaget had worked for Compagne Français of Paris. Pastilles and gums were monopolised by the French and any British firm able to make products of comparable quality but at a lower price might gain an advantage. The cost of boiling pans needed for their manufacture was much lower than in the case of the Van Houten cocoa press. Joseph Rowntree was insistent upon having products of unrivalled quality and at first refused Gaget's early samples made at Tanners Moat. It was not until two years later, in 1881, that the firm manufactured 'Fruit Pastilles'. They were sold loose and unadvertised in 4lb boxes. The crystallised gums and pastilles sold retail for a penny an ounce. The firm was still making a loss in the 1880s and suffered a severe blow in 1883 when Henry Isaac died suddenly of peritonitis. Joseph was now left on his own to run an ailing business. The saviour of the company was Claude Gaget, whose pastilles gradually brought about a permanent improvement in the fortunes of the firm. By 1885 4 tonnes of these sweets were manufactured every week and the work force increased to 200.

Two years later, a horse drawn Rulley carried the daily output to the station. Tanners Moat works was still very ramshackle and unsuited to large scale production, adjoining cottages and stables extended the original premises.

Possibly under the influence of his son, John William, who began work at the factory in 1885 at the age of seventeen, Joseph dropped his earlier opposition to advertising and in 1886 discreet notices commending Rowntrees Confectionery appeared in the popular magazines, 'Tit-Bits' and 'Answers'. Between 1883 and 1886 the firm's annual sales doubled to £110,000. A nine foot replica of a tin of Elect cocoa had for some time been mounted on a touring delivery cart pulled by a pony. The first marketing initiative of 1897 involved its transfer to a motor car that travelled the North of England. It attracted attention wherever it went. It was Joseph's second son, Arnold's first venture into mass advertising. Arnold Rowntree's next venture was equally dramatic, at the Oxford versus Cambridge Boat Race in 1897, a barge covered with adverts for 'Elect Cocoa' and drawn by mechanically propelled swans sailed majestically down the course. It was definitely noticeable. Joseph might have winced if he had seen it, but he remained true to his long established policy of never interfering, if he could avoid it, in the activities of those to whom he had entrusted a job.

Joseph also began negotiations with a Dutchman, Cornelius Hollander. He disliked Hollander's continuous haggling and search for guarantees, seeing it as a challenge to his own reputation and honesty. He remained insistent that once Hollander had produced a cocoa equal to Van Houten pure essence, he should reveal the process to him. After several years, it was obvious that Hollander knew less about the Van Houten method than he had stated.

Elect cocoa, now a pure essence, was finally re-launched in August 1887, seven years after its original launch in 1880, when it failed and had to be withdrawn. Hollander worked behind closed doors in the North Street building and the knowledge of his experiments was hidden from Joseph Rowntree and his staff. Eventually Hollander's intractability, and a suspicion that he was charging the firm too much for his materials, was the cause of unbearable tension. One day Hollander was locked out and his workroom broken open. The 'Secret' was out.

Joseph's interests lay with the welfare and morale of his work force. He was more and more concerned about the growing polarization between capital and labour and the alienation of employers in large industrial organisations like his own. Even in the 1890s, it could still be said that for many manufacturers, labour was just a factor, a commodity to be bought and sold in accordance with the hagglings of the market. That it was housed in a human body and impelled by a human soul, were no more than accidental factors which had no bearing on its usefulness. Such an attitude could only be abhorrent to a man like Joseph Rowntree, to whom individuals were always persons first and employees afterwards. In an effort to bridge the gap between the management and the employees, he set up the 'Cocoa Worker Magazine', one of the first in house journals in Britain. He hoped that it would help to hold employees' interest in their work.

In 1890 Rowntrees bought 29 acres of land on Haxby Road, on the North East of the city, and set about building a new factory which would be light, airy and spacious.

The move from Tanners Moat began five years later and was not completed until 1910. Joseph Rowntrees most ambitious welfare project was the creation of New Earswick village on 123 acres of land which was adjoining the factory. The architect was Raymond Unwin, a pioneer in town planning and the garden village concept. There would be no more than twelve houses to the acre, each must have a garden with two fruit trees, and all living rooms must face south making full use of the sun. Among the stipulations made in the deed, was that none of the buildings in the village should be used for the manufacture, distribution or sale of intoxicating liquor.

In a referendum held in the village in 1978, 87 per cent voted in favour of allowing alcohol to be sold in the Folk Hall. Joseph's wish was not respected.

In 2007 Tescos applied for a licence to sell alcohol at their shop near George Cadburys village of Bournville and was turned down.

In the centre of the photograph is the 'Elephant and Castle' in Skeldergate where a young Joseph Rowntree and a friend called James Backhouse went to an auction in 1822. They managed to sober up the auctioneer enough to conduct his business. 28 The Pavement became the elder Josephs property. James Backhouse was one of two Quaker brothers who owned a nursery on Toft Green. They became very successful and outgrew their premises, they were only too glad to accept an offer of £5,700 for it from George Hudson so he could build his Railway station within the city walls.

The shop with the fanlight above the doors is Rowntrees shop in The Pavement. It would be nice to think the gentleman standing in the doorway is the young Joseph Rowntree. At the present time it is the Pizza Hut in The Pavement.

The building on the right with the bracket lamp was purchased by the Retreat in 1810 for patients in least need of confinement, used as a Quaker boarding school for boys from 1823–1845. Photo taken in 1860, the small arch to the right of the bar has been demolished, the large arch in situ today was built in 1862. The Headmaster was William Simpson, the next Headmaster was to be John Ford.

At quarterly meeting it was decided to buy Sir John Armstrongs house in Bootham known as Lady Armstrong's Mansion, including six acres of land for £4,500 of which £1,563 was recovered by the sale of some land to York Asylum. The above building on the left was to become Bootham School. John Ford realising he would be asked to be Superintendent, without the responsibility of ownership, gladly acceded to the request, officiated with great wisdom until 1865. Another reason to move was the pungent disease ridden swamp behind Lawrence Street, the remains of the Kings Pool on Foss Islands.

At school in 1848 Joseph on extreme left, Henry Isaac on extreme right.
When Joseph was 14 and brother John was 16 they went to Ireland with their father and headmaster John Ford. His father told them to take their botanical cases and notebooks. Joseph saw the horrors of the Irish potato famine which influenced his thinking until the end of his days. It is probable that the two men on some sort of commission for the Society of Friends with a view to starting relief work.

BOOTHAM SCHOOL, YORK.   A STUDY OF POND LIFE.   *Exhibited at the Franco-British Exhibition, 1908*

The great fire at Bootham School in 1899 caused considerable damage, the gymnasium and laboratory were completely wrecked. Later the same day, headmaster John Frith Fryer tendered his immediate resignation. The school moved to premises in Scarborough, used by Olivers Mount School which had recently closed. Despite many inconveniences this episode of Bootham-by-the-Sea was recalled with happy memories by all who experienced it. The headmaster was Arthur Rowntree who took over at Bootham when they returned in January 1902. The fire was caused by a pupil boiling snail shells, in adult life he became a farmer and blew himself up while trying to remove a tree stump with dynamite. His name believe it or not was Impey White.

Tukes shop at the corner of Castlegate and Coppergate prior to demolition.

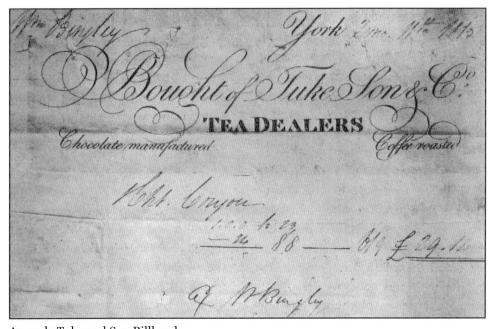

An early Tuke and Son Billhead.

The apprentices who lived above the shop in The Pavement.
Joseph Rowntree in the centre, George Cadbury is on the right, at the back grocers all with no thoughts as yet on chocolate, who would have believed what lay ahead.

Adult school in Hope Street in Walmgate.
John Stephenson Rowntree first met his class on January 20th 1856. Joseph Rowntree senior was present at that meeting.

When Joseph Rowntree II was teaching at Hope Street he decided to separate the adults from the children who were a bit disruptive. The rented premises above in Lady Peckitts Yard behind The Pavement shop was the first of many adult schools.

The Women's Class in Lady Peckitts Yard.

The 'A' Class in Lady Peckitts Yard.

The Rowntree brothers opened an adult school in every district in York. I have a photographic record of those schools, I have restricted the photographs as the story is about Rowntrees cocoa works. I have also written a book on the Rowntree village of New Earswick published by William Sessions.

A splendid view of the Tanners Moat factory from the river
The chairman of the York Water Company about to board the River King going to open
the new water treatment plant on Acomb Landing.
Note the band on board.

Henry Isaacs Cocoa Works at Tanners Moat. Joseph's office was above the sign on the left. He had a trap door, he use to open it and ask staff to take the post to Lendal.

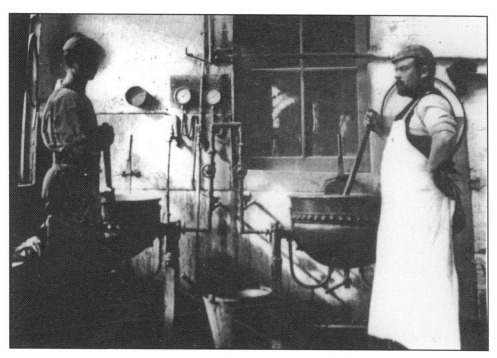

The days boiling for pastilles which saved the Rowntree factory from going under.

Moulding Chocolates in Tanners Moat in 1890.

Weighing pastilles which were
sold in 3 pound boxes.

The complete male workforce at Tanners Moat.

Top Row: J.W. Danby, H Sidney, J.J. Robinson

Second Row: J. Clayton, S. Walker, S. Mitchel, T. Pulon, R. Lowe, W. Cook, F. Dixon,
              J. Scaife

Third Row: J. Pecket, C. Carmichael, Claude Gaget The Saviour of Rowntrees
              presenting something to A. Bland, S.C. Hanks, W. Henderson, C. Turner

Seated: J. Archer, Capt. Smith, T. Walls, J. Myton, W. Pinder, G. Harriner,
              C. Hanks, T. Muldowney, F. Smith, G. Barker, J. Watson, T. Penrose

Mr William Laykock with his Rulley taking the days production to the railway station.
He started at the N.E.R in 1868, he reckons he was Rowntree staff except Fridays when
his wages came from the North Eastern Railway Company. He collected from Rowntrees
from 1877 until his death in 1911.

The extra premises purchase in North Street for expansion due to the popularity of pastilles.

Wright & Rich of 132 Milk Street, Boston. Henry Isaacs agent in America.

The new factory in Haxby Road, light and airy with lots of garden space, a far cry from Tanners Moat.

Mixed staff enjoy a game of tennis on the lawns at the factory, there was also a bowling green.

Girls dance class on the lawns.

The boys give a PT display to visitors at the cocoa works.

The girls west dining room in 1906.

The girls restroom in 1906. These girls had their wicker baskets long before the Sloane Rangers.

Seebohm Rowntree's book on poverty had shown the unemployed, the old, the very young and the sick made up the majority of those in poverty and it was with the old the Joseph had concerned himself. In 1904 he appointed a committee to explore the question of a pension fund. This was a new idea in the world of business and a committee took two years to work out how it could best be done. It was of necessity very expensive Seebohm, writing of its establishment, said many firms may hesitate to adopt a pension scheme on this account, but it is probable that those firms carry a heavy cost in 'hidden pensions' without realising the fact. If a firm establishes a liberal pension scheme it will doubtless that at the same time fix a definite retirement age, and will in itself never find itself with a number of old workers of low working capacity drawing full pay, such employees are very costly; not only does the firm lose on them individually but their presence tend to lower the pace and lessen the output of the whole shop. They are kept on because they have worked faithfully for a great number of years and the management does not care do dismiss them.

When Rowntrees pension scheme began the state old age pension was two years away, the state pension was 5 shillings a week the princely some of 25 pence, it could not be drawn by anyone with an income of 10 shillings or more and could not be claimed until the recipient was 70 years old.

Joseph gave £10,000 out of his own pocket to the pension scheme when it first started, the company gave £9,000. These were large sums for the time and they enabled the scheme to start on a solvent basis and also provide for those employees who were due to retire soon after it was established. Josephs aim was to establish a pension at least equal to half a mans wage that he was earning at retirement. The company paid in 30 shillings for every 20 shillings paid by men and 60 shillings for 20 shillings paid in by women. Although they had no pattern to guide them, the men who formulated the pension scheme at Rowntrees showed uncanny vision in working out its details. The foundation upon which they built was so basically sound that most of their ideas have survived intact to the present day.

The first pension fund trustees.

Left to right: J. Brownilow, J.B. Morrell, B.S. Rowntree, Joseph Rowntree, E.R. Cross,
W. Fox, T. H. Appleton, S.H. Sidney and A. Wilkinson.

Girls domestic class.

Statuette used to meet visitors to the cocoa works, and deftly peel off the postcard shown for the visitors.

Centre background: Harry Hudson, Alf Moses, Walter Raw, Albert Raw and Fred Danby.

Foreground: Jack Wrigglesworth and Charlie Shaw the others have not been identified.

Building a great name 1904 erecting the giant letters on the block, each letter is 10 feet high from the 'R' in Rowntrees to the 'A' in cocoa is 112 feet.

Dining room kitchens of yesterday situated on three floors of the cake department. Photo taken 1898

Centre: Chef Jack Crosby who was a fireman at the time of his retirement.

Bertha busy making cakes in the new dining block alas a private hospital. She is still using tables from original kitchen.

Before Yearsley baths opened the bed of the River Foss was flagged and used as an open air pool. It was situated behind Yearsley Crescent. The fever hospital can be seen in the background. The pool was used after Yearsley baths opened, being that it was free.

Some of the dignitaries who attended the opening ceremony of the City of York Yearsley baths, which was given to the city by Joseph Rowntree.

The opening ceremony just after Joseph Rowntree had handed over the keys.

These adults are not fishing for children, this was the method used at the time to keep them afloat during swimming lessons.

Fancy Diving Prohibited. The baths closed on 9th July 2007 for a complete refurbishment which will take 3 months to complete.

Are the non swimmers keeping a lookout for the attendant whilst one of the swimmers executes a fancy dive.

Dressed in their familiar overalls they conduct thousands of visitors around the works last year 1926. The total shown around the works was 40,000.

Travellers of 1910 – Renshaw, Eastwood, Bromilow, Kidd, Hall, Ward,
Robinson, Farrow, Brown,
Varney, Watkinson, Greir, Thorne, Helliwell.

The Post Office Flying Squad – D. Blaker, A. Benson, M. Heselwood, H. Lowther,
M. Pocock, I. Collyer, N. Binns, D. Press, F. Seaton, G. Orr.

London Depot
Inset – Mr Cowling.

Various modes of lorries in this fine view of the transport section. Note the steam lorry on the left, open cab lorries with solid tyres, when you think they delivered by donkey cart at Tanners Moat they have come a long way.

Pneumatic tyres, Plain Mr York livery and splendid uniforms for the drivers.

Packing tins of chocolates for the troops in South Africa during the Boer War.

Packing special boxes and tins for the Coronation of King Edward VII.

The above and next three photographs were all taken on the Rowntree Estate in Dover Jamaica.

Sorting dried cocoa beans by hand.

The husking house.

The garden party at the cocoa works in August 1906. The band competition had its entrants, there were also many entrants in the horticultural competitions.

The cocoa works photographers at Malham Cove.

Garden party in The Homestead in aid of The York Childrens Home at Kirk Hammerton.

York cocoa works show and contest 1907.

Advertising Rowntrees elect cocoa on a Thames barge during the 1899 boat race, Hungerford bridge can be seen in the background.

The elect cocoa car when it was being driven in Middlesborough, being top heavy it blew over causing quite a stir.

A magnificent advert for Rowntrees motoring chocolate.

An Elect poster of 1910.

Rowntree Fire engines at Crystal Palace 1905.

Fire engines in 1905.

The Rowntrees steam fire engine.

FIRE AT MESSRS WALES & SON OGLEFORTH. ARRIVAL OF ROWNTREE'S FIRE BRIGADE.

The same engine attending a fire at Wales' Garage in Ogleforth, the same garage is now in the Castle Museum.

New motor fire engine, July 1912.

Cleaning up the old Sam Mason steam fire engine which is to be presented to the Castle Museum.

Fireman of 1894

Standing: W. Lawrence, T. Odd, T. Lisle, T. Penrose, W. Wilson, A. Illingworth, E. Hawksby, F. Brown, W. Welborn, J. Sharpley, T. Tindall and W. Daniels.

On ladder: G. Methell, J. Crosby, H. Borwell and G. Coult.

At this time Rowntrees only supplied tunics and helmets hence the odd trousers.

The Lord Mayor's Parade 1928. Lendal Bridge in background, tram waiting to come out of Rougier Street, Rowntrees horse drawn steam fire engine on the left, the new super white fire engine second on the right.

Fire brigade on their 55 BHP Dennis.

The new Dennis fire engine. The engine develops 75 horse power and pumps water at 600 gallons per minute.

Australian womens cricket team fraternise with the cocoa worker team.

The Middlesborough football team on Rowntrees pride and joy their new fire engine.

Girls cycle race sports day 1905.

Rowntrees Railway Team
A. Nichols (Coach), F. Pierpoint, W. Whitehead, T. Herridge, J. Mills, M. Flatley (Coach)
E.G. Rayson, J.E. Smith, J. Cox, F. Barton.

The Waverley Bag Room outing to Castle Howard.
A party of 60 met in College Street, 38 boarded Char-a-bancs and the rest cycled. A visit to the castle by kind permission of Lady Carlisle was enjoyed by all.

The Cocoa Works Angling Club

Amongs the many faces were: F. Metcalf, S. Smith, A.J. Avdaer, J. Simpson,
E. Daniels, C. Humpherson

A. Harrison, J.T. Ridsdale, J. Walker, A. Sherwood, A. Moses, F. Kirby, F. Brown

C. Robinson, A. Lawrence, H. Willis, A. Rudd, W. Harvey, H. Holt, J. Sutcliffe

W. Welbourne, W. Rush, G. Russell, W. Bolton, J. Pullon, C. Watkinson, T. Gott and
W. Morley.

Cake Department Angling Club in Exhibition Square on their way to Sutton on Derwent

Names of the above company

A. Welborn, F. Henderson, A. Newlove, W.A. Welborn, W. Frankish, E. Key, J. McNally,
C. Musgrove, H. Marsden, F. Ward, E. Daw, B. Lawton and A.S. Wheldon.

Note the Sheppee steam char-a-banc these were built at the Sheppee factory in
Lawrence Street, York.

Netball Team 1935-36.
Phyllis Rennison, Betty Foster, Ethel Travis, Marrion Heppell, Zena Flower and Betty Smith.

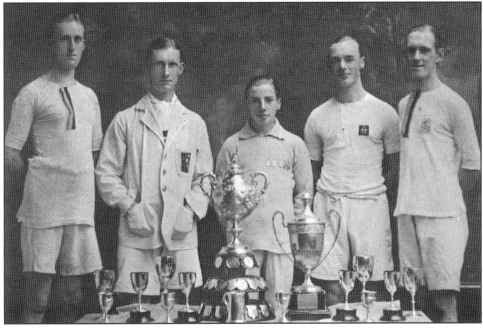

1920 Senior 4 Crew – A. Hall Yorkshire Insurance Company, F. Bell, S. Smithers and L. Weatherley all of Rowntree and Company and W. Peat LNER.

The departmental trophy winners 1906

R. Tindale, J. Mills, S. Atkinson, R. Hawks, C. Mercer and J. Rogers
W. Hawsley, A. Thrackrah, T. Hope, W. Goodson, E. Hudson and W. Varlow.

Shenton McGregor, Rose Finlayson, Smailes, Mowsley, Randles, C. Fanthorpe, G. Ward
McAllen, J.H.Ping, Maw

Brown, H. Bullock, D.S. Crighton, fearne, Hurworth.

Cake Room winners of the departmental competition

Back: J. Drinkel, Satchwell, Stubbs, Campy, Haxby, Yoward and S. Harrison
Middle: Butler, Crombie, Baines, Titley, Lickiss and Simpson
Front: Bradley, Todd, Newlove, Sunderland and Plain Mr York

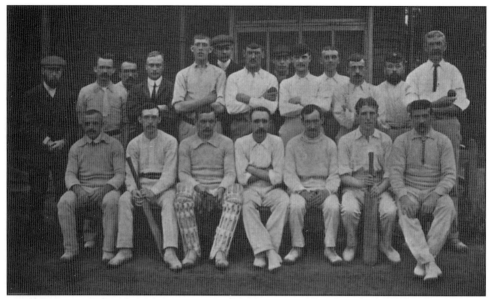

Standing: G. Boyce, E. Dearlove, D.S.Crighton, T.H. Spetch, F. Hields, G.R.Lee, T. Herridge, P. Utley, E. Hepworth, T. Bramley, G. Smith, W. Boyce, F. Lazenby

Sitting: J. Hill, J. Fearn, T. Bellerby, H. Wilknson, H. Routhwaite, W. Hotham, S. Childs.

A Bowling Club Group of 1905

H. Holt, C. Walker, J. Woodcock
J.S. Eastwood, W. Beaumonts,
T. Douglas, J. Sunderland,
A. Pattie, F. Tindale, J. Cooke,
G. Dawson, G. Parker,
E. Grantham, E. Pauw,
J. Howard and J. Sanger.

The York and District First Division Shield donated by Rowntree and Company in the season 1901-2. The cocoa works team won it in its first year. They did not win it again until 1931 by the team shown above.

Early photograph of the cocoa works from the air. The library and the theatre have not yet been built. The streets bottom left have been airbrushed out and replaced with mature trees and grassland.

Bottom Tennis Courts Dining block, the library opposite, White Cross Lodge once home to the Chief Constable Haley, hence Haleys Terrace and then open air swimming pool. It is under a full refurbishment at the present time 2007. There are plans for celebrations for its Centenary in 2008.

Staff waiting to go on shift.
Nice view of the dining block and White Cross Lodge.

Haxby Road Military Hospital (Rowntrees dining block, York). At the present time 2007 it is now a Nuffield Hospital.

One of the wards showing the casualties of the First World War.

Waving greetings to the men with the colours. As a picture postcard it was sent to all fellow workers who enlisted in the 1914-18 war.

The message on the card read 'The Almond paste and office girls defy the German submarines.'

Doctor Peter MacDonald who married Joseph Rowntrees' daughter Agnes Julia, provided the medical care at the factory in the company's time.

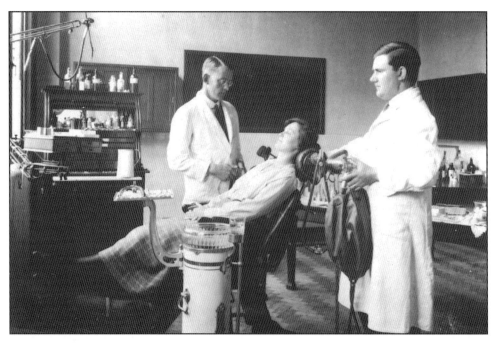

Doctor MacDonald also suggested that bad teeth led to ill health, a dentist was duly employed. Such provision improved the well-being of employees and reduce the hours lost through ill health.

The rush hour on the bridge before its widening causes a bottleneck on Haxby Road.

Cyclists and pedestrians took their lives in their own hands.

Mr Joss shows the girls gardening class, how it should be done. I like the style of the girl on the right. She must have practiced leaning on the spade.

Goodbye summer, the dinner hour girls are interested in Isaac and his mechanical leaf sweeper.

Joy Hudson, Louie Stirk, Bessie Christon and Janet Dobson pose with a prize ram at the Yorkshire Show at Hull where they were in charge of the Rowntree kiosk.

Taken during the Prince of Wales visit in addition to playing many engagements and competitions they were awarded second prize at the Kippax competition.

Plain Mr York of York Yorks visited a Canadian orphanage in a stage coach. He distributed bars of chocolate to the children in the Montreal orphanage.

A unique group: Mrs Wood 39 years service, Barwick 29 years, Myers 32 years,
Miss N Loftus 28 years, Miss E. Nenton 28 years, Miss L Sunman 26
years and Miss a Gilligan 31 years. All experience in hand covering and
marking chocolates. Mrs Wood taught these ladies to cover 28 years
before photo was taken.

The Lena Ashwell Players advertised at York Theatre Royal in 1928.

The Lena Ashwell Players who appeared at the Joseph Rowntree Theatre, posed on the lawns at the cocoa works.

The Lord Mayor presents prizes to our Sea Cadets who won the Open Sculling Races organized by the Ouse Boat Club.

Saying it in Chinese, Rowntree advert over a shop in Hong Kong.

Plain Mr York in good company. Rowntrees chocolates well to the front during Civic Week in Newcastle, New South Wales.

A study in expressions, children thought Plain Mr York of York Yorks was great fun.

An Elect cocoa demonstration in the Matsuya store in Tokyo.

At the opening of the Joseph Rowntree Theatre.

From left to right: Mrs Seebohm Rowntree Sheriff, C.F. Anderson, Mr Seebohm
Rowntree, Lord Mayor W.H. Shaw, his wife Mrs N.H. Shaw,
Sheriffs Lady Mrs C.F. Anderson, Mayor of Harrogate S. Cartwright.

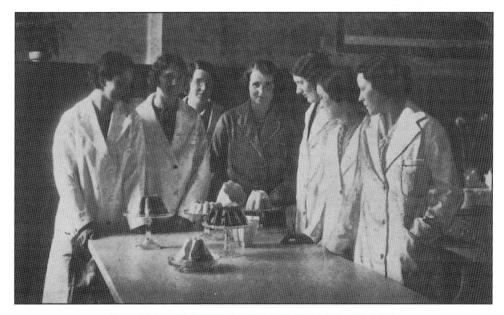

DEMONSTRATORS FOR JELLY AND COCOA
V. Long, D. Winskill, M. Alexandra, O. Gillance, G. Sutcliffe, D. Milner and M. Trotter.

Looking through my William Hayes Collection I came across this photograph at Barmoor 1925. On closer inspection I saw it was Joseph Rowntree, his son Arnold on the left and some of his grandchildren and great grandchildren. As the great man died in March of that year it is possible it is the last photographic image. On Monday 2nd March 1925 the Northern edition of the Daily Mirror carried on its front page a photograph of crowds of people walking past a newly made grave, the caption was funeral of Mr Joseph Rowntree of York. It covered the whole page, there was just room for an announcement in small type to say New York was shaken by an earthquake. The man whose death in his eighty-ninth year was considered more significant than an earthquake.

General view of the Sawmill interior.

New borehole near Rowntree halt sunk into the sandstone to a depth of 400 feet. A tube 30 inch in diameter will enable water to be pumped at 50,000 gallons per minute at a pressure of 70lb per square inch.

Father Christmas about to start a special mission which will bring joy to hundreds of children.

Special Christmas Gift Box.

Nigerian representative Mr T. Spiers presented this handsome brass casket of gums to two ruling Chiefs Sarnin Donra and Sarnin Katsina.

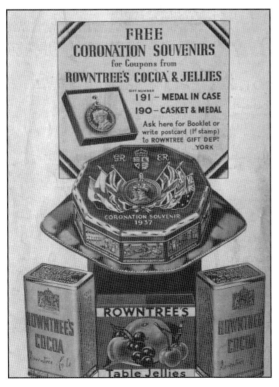

The coupons scheme was a great incentive for people to save coupons to redeem them for a free gift. According to the numbers on the photograph there must have been a large selection.

Handmade boxes are filled with special chocolates. I think the girls wanted to be in the photograph.

Hand feeding chocolate bars into the foil wrapping machine. Note they were also taken off by hand.

Any more for Scarborough. The War Memorial party in Exhibition Square, 200 people wives and children whose husbands were lost in the First World War.

CAKE MOULDERS' PICNIC PARTY

Back: G. Tomlinson, C. Cole, H. Low, C. Morrell, Mrs Grantham, N. Severs, L. Harrison, L. Horwell and A. Headley

Middle: S. Plume, A. Greenwood, Mrs Sunman, Mrs Fenwick, Mrs Scott, A. Usher, E. Walsham, A. Phillips and L. Deighton

Front: M. Barrett, L. Newton, Mrs Brown, O. Knaggs, M. Wragg, P. Harrison and L. Proud.

Duchess of Yorks visit in 1927.

The Black Boy Chocolate Kabin in Coney Street, York.
During the depression Cadbury and Fry cut their prices, the Rowntree subsidiary Black Boy shops could not make a profit, asking Rowntree for a reduction, were told 'we make a quality product at a fair price'. Rowntree later compensated Black Boy shareholders from its own funds, it soon took steps to sell the firm to another multiple retailer Maynards.

Gracie Fields taken at the opening of a large cinema in Middlesex.

George Formby's better half got the bigger box.

MISS RENEE KELLY
leading actress in "The Heart of a Child," "playing" at work in the factory

(1) "Clocking In" (2) Weighing Gums. (3) Packing Chocolates

It took me a long time to collect the three postcards that made up the top photograph.

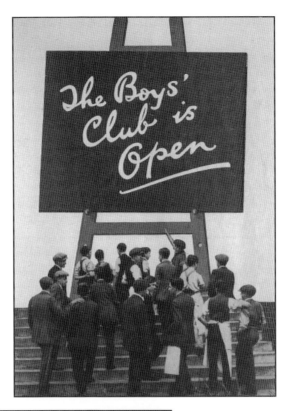

Loading up for the boys camp.
It looks as though they took
everything but the kitchen sink, by
the looks of the van it would not
have surprised me if they didn't take
that as well.

Boys camp in the Lake District at Watendlath Bridge.

Boy camp in the Lake District at Ashness Bridge.

Boys club visit to the Minster in 1909.

Pulling the Rowntrees barge out of The Foss basin at Blue Bridge Lane.

Many hands make light work of getting the barge shipshape and ready to sail.

Joseph Rowntree greets the Prince of Wales the future King Edward VIII who later abdicated.

Joseph Rowntree and Mary Astor in the garden at Haxby Road when she visited the factory.

The Royal party at the Card Box Hill.

Front Row: Mr B.S. Rowntree, H.R.H. Queen Mary, Princess Royal, Mr G.S. Crossley

Back Row: Mr G.J. Harris, Earl of Harwood and his two sons.

Back Row: Mr A.S. Rowntree, Lord Nunburnholme, Sir Hugh Bell and
Wing Commander Greig

Front Row: Archbishop of York, Duke of York, B.S. Rowntree and Lord Harewood.

This photograph of girls on an Aero wrapping machine appeared in the National Press in 1940.

The Melangeur Department, where all the chocolate is mixed.

The Moulding Room in 1940.

Mr R. Staveley and his staff, 1912

J. Woodcock, W. Limbert, J. Hardcastle, E. Hendry, J. Smith, F. Kirlew, J. Holder,
W. Howard, P. Grundon, R. Pinder, W. Bullock, F. Garnett, R. Moore, W. Limbert,
J. Evans, G. Wood, G. Backhouse, J. Neale, J. Wright, W. Bardy, F. Hornby, J. Hendry,
W. Andrews, J. Rankin, J. Wadsworth, R. Staveley, J. Bardy, J. Garbutt, A. Gee,
E. Humphrey, H. Nekervis and F. Smith.

Day Continuation School netball at York City football ground.

Day Continuation Class youths gym class.

Anderson shelter prior to being buried underground.

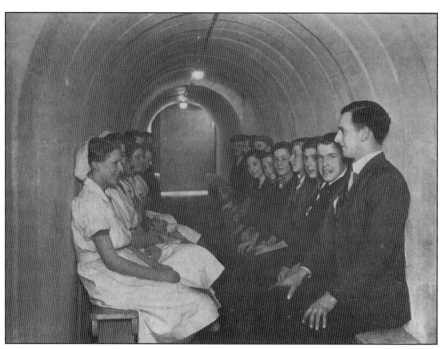

Inside one of the new shelters in the orchard.

No 3 Section Rescue Squad.

Top: G. Allison, S. Barnett, J. Hanson, W. Howe, H. Wells, B.G. Walker,
W. Tolliday, H. Shortle

Bottom: J. Warriner, A. Hudson, A.R. Minney (Leader), A. Pratt, G. Richman

The cocoa works home guard set up a road block between the cocoa works and New
Earswick, no wonder we could all sleep safely in our beds with these chaps to look after
us.

COUNTY INDUSTRIES LTD.. YORK
MARCH 1943

Setup at the factory to produce fuses to be used in armaments for the war effort, very much against Quaker thinking but forced upon them by the Government.

Entering the fuse making plant one had to leave their contraband ie. cigarettes and matches.

Girls assembling and filling fuses, after work they had to go to the dirty area remove clothing, shower then go off to the clean area to get changed to go home. On entering, the procedure was reversed.

Filling the last fuse to come off the assembly line no. 7,809,579.

A great effort by all staff during the war.

PRE-WAR
2

OVER 7.500.000 TINS

OVER 9.0000.000 TINS

VARIED activities were carried on under the old name of "Cream Department." These ranged from the packing of more than 9 million tins of dried egg and 7½ million tins of household milk, so much appreciated by every housewife in the country, to the assembling and despatching of over 4 million anti-tank mine fuses. In February 1941, after the heavy bombing of Birmingham when the Ryvita factory there was destroyed, part of its manufacture was transferred to the Cream Department.

WAR-TIME

N.M.U. 15.

The Northern Motoring Union which looked after Rowntrees transport. The driver Harry Hawley was an air raid warden, he was on duty in Tang Hall Lane he shouted at a motorist to dip his headlamps, a soldier on leave said 'I will stop him'. He drew a revolver and accidentally shot Harry who died from his wounds.

Part of the railway staff 1912

Back: W. Wood, J. Ringrose, A. Bradley, G.R. Lee, A. Precious, J. Anderson, R. Burton.

Middle: C. Garnett, A.E. Harrison, A. Clark, E.V. Hartley, T. Wardle, E.W. Wilson, A.G. Simpson.

Front: C.J.S. Boyce, P. Padley, H. Long, G. Massey, E.G. Raison, A. Hall, A.E. Oglesby, A.J. Strickland.

A Bradford excursion train bound for the cocoa works. Photographed at Birkenshaw Station.

Loading cocoa at Rowntrees private railway station.

A consignment of fruit for Rowntrees pastilles and fruit gums. Is their any wonder they were best sellers when you think of the 'e' numbers used in this day and age 2007.

Goods train at Rowntrees Halt in 1956.

Rowntrees workers board the Selby train on their journey home.

Girls from the cream packing on an outing to the West Riding to do some charity work during WWII.

ROWNTREE ARGOSY SEA RANGER REPRESENTATIVES AT THE SILVER JUBILEE CELEBRATIONS AT WINDSOR CASTLE

Miss M. Hall, Miss J. Lisle, Miss D. Rainey and Miss M. Dalby.

Grand Finale 'Swiss Family Robinson' Christmas 1945.

Rowntree employees in York Thanksgiving Week Procession.

Workers playtime at the Joseph Rowntree Theatre.
George Middleton at the piano, Jean Inglis, Beryl Orde and Jack Warner.

Rowntree Band marching past the saluting base in front of the Mansion House 1946.

B.B.C. Northern Orchestra, Conductor Charles Groves, in the Rowntree Theatre.

The export drive 1947.

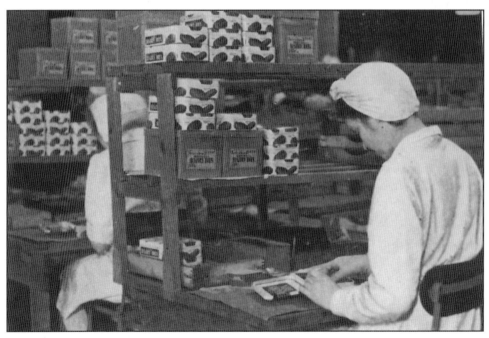

Export drive 1947, a small portion of the cocoa works activities to sell merchandise to hard currency areas in particular and to other countries in general.

Mrs Webster and Mrs Hardacre packing foiled sweets for export.

Noel Daniels and Tom Elleker who finish off the cartons ready for dispatch to the store room.

A chocoholics dream Easter present.

Office messengers Silver Jubilee 1925-1950.

Back: Pamela Dickson, Patricia Pilcher, Patricia Beckett, Mary Smith, Enid Maw, Jean Hempsall

Front: Audrey Burbridge, Shirley Lister, Audrey Hullatt, Morag Macneil, Beryl Harrison.

Rowntrees delivering to the Queen Mary.

Mr Wallace the Chairman visiting the Arts & Craft exhibition at the cocoa works.

Henry Leethams flour mill on the banks of the Foss in Hungate. He built a huge warehouse on the Foss it was part of the largest flour mill in Europe. The warehouse was designed by Walter Penty. It consisted of 5 storeys plus a 9 storey water tower. Rowntree took over the warehouse in 1937 for the storage of cocoa beans.

Nice view of Wormaldscut on the right constructed in 1794 in order to serve Samuel Wormalds brewery and timber yard at the rear of Walmgate. Wormald became very successful he was able to move to a large house in Bootham a more fitting address for one who was to become Lord Mayor in 1809.

Unloading a barge at Rowntrees Wharfe on the River Foss. Half a million pounds was ear marked for a chocolate museum on the ground floor when it was converted to flats but the idea was not implemented.

The Foss was always prone to flooding. Here an ex-military vehicle a D.U.K.W was used to ferry goods. The Foss barrier at St Georges Field has now cured this problem.

Fred Littlewood is feeding the elevator and Tommy Hampton is taking off and piling.

Herbert Clitheroe and Charlie Turpin load export cases. Jim Baxter and driver Carney get the next cases ready.

Packers of 1893. George Shepherd on the left in the Billy cock hat, also in the photograph are G. Howard, J. Akers and T. Barrowby.

Tom McNamara and Ted Bolton checking assembly of orders for van delivery.

Fred Dixon and Harry Gill load a container for dispatch by steamer to our Belfast depot.

Inspecting gum Arabic.

F. Chown, J. Coates, T. Burner.

The gum department came into being in 1879 when Joseph Rowntree engaged the French confectioner Claude Gaget at Tanners Moat. Production began early 1890s.

Depositing gums and pastilles.
G. Barker, J. Neale and H. Gell.

Stacking pastilles, Freda Imeson and Audrey Dalton.

Packing tubes of pastilles by hand.

Arthur Barkway, Alf Moses and Les Allison building baffle wall on Super Heater No 8 Adamson boiler.

Arthur Goddard and 'Peg' Lightfoot trowelling pyrofugent floor in the cream department.

Les Dove, Bill Bushell, Arthur Birkenshaw, Jim Hull and Ted Dalton working in the joiners shop.

Walt Howe, Syd Carter, George Smith and Ronald Long on a removal job on the roof of the new cream extension block.

Bill Arnot busy on mould assembly in the mould shop.

Malcolm Cox repairs a boiling pan
sheet metal workers shop.

Fred Burley (Striker) and Jack Bardy (Blacksmith) making a light forging.

Walter Taylor and Eric Redpath cutting deals.

George Watkinson and Albert Elliott operating case nailing machines with Fred Chaplin transporting.

Arthur Archer working on an advertising display, The White Rose of York. A Rowntree Elect cocoa label of 1881 is in the centre of the display.

Edward Drinkel packing a case for Himalayan expedition going to the base camp for the attempt on Mount Everest in 1953.

Printing office, upwards of 6,500 copies of printed material are turned out in a year. Photo 1928.

Some of the Post Office staff in 1952.

Harold Deighton and Harry Dinsdale of the sales department 1952. Their combined service with the company totals 92 years.

Daphne Woods sales statistics sorting cards from which invoices have been prepared. These cards are then tabulated to give total sales of each Rowntree line.

A general view of the wages paying office 1952.

Flo Davidson and Mary Ventress studying the income tax charts before entering 'how much' on each personal wages and tax record card.

A corner of the new club room in the dining block. Alas it is a private hospital.

FOOD GOOD AFTER 50 YEARS

ANTARCTIC SUPPLIES TESTED

Tins of food about 50 years old taken from the Antarctic bases of Shackleton and Scott were opened at the British Food Manufacturing Industries Research Association's laboratories at Leatherhead, Surrey, yesterday.

Tests were made on a tin of kippered herrings, one of lunch tongue, and a half pound tin of cocoa from a depôt of the 1908-09 Shackleton expedition; a tin of pea-flour for making soup from the Cape Evans depôt of the 1911 Scott expedition; and a bottle of chutney and a tin of meat extract from the United States 1939-41 expedition.

Only once was one of the tasters heard to express disapproval as a tin was opened, and that was for the newest, the meat extract. The 50-year-old herring and tongue proved quite edible, although the herring were a little "mushy," because of being thrown around. Verdicts on the tongue ranged from "Not at all bad" to "rather cheesy." The pea flour "could still be used as the basis of soup." The chutney was praised and the cocoa was pronounced "excellent."

All the 50-year-old tins were air-tight. None of them had been lacquered inside, though the outsides were protected by red oxide of iron.

An extract from The Times Newspaper.

Back Row: *left to right:* M. Robertson, A. Stamp, L. Bilham, R. King, N. Kilvington.

Third Row: *left to right:* E. A. Sutton, W. Wreghitt, R. Wrigglesworth, W. Medley, H. Humphrey.

Second Row: *left to right:* G. Hurst, D. B. Ives, R. Bilham, P. Morimer, L. Lambeth, E. Pratt, D. Oakes, D. Bilham, E. Dobson.

Front: *left to right:* R. Stamp, M. Castro and K. Stamp.

'1066 and all that' performed in 1944.

'The Boy Friend' performed in 1961.

From the Black and White Minstrel Show 1963.

Mr Jack Ringrose of the architects department built his own bungalow at Osbaldwick, it took him 2 years, 1 to accumulate the materials and 1 to build. He is seen above with his wife Molly.

Junior Course of 1956

Back: John Kilvington, Michael McLeod, Peter Ferguson, Ronald Helstrip, David Micklethwaite, John Eastwood, Barry Payne.

Middle: Edward Henderson, Alan Smythe, Howard Marshall, John Boyne, Charles Hutchinson, Peter Kirby, David Rhodes.

Front: Robert Hill, Michael Hancock, Barry Clifford, Colin Simmons, Alwyne Pearson, Terrence Dodsworth, Ronald Judson

This is the last photograph I have included. The Cocoa Works Magazine and later the Rowntrees Newspaper continues in the same format in to work teams and new junior courses for young men and women joining the works.

Bibliography

Crane, H.	1969	Sweet Encounter
Knapp, A.W.	1920	Cocoa and Chocolate
Melling, J.	1979	British Employers and the Development of Industrial Welfare State 1880–1920
Othic, J.	1976	The Cocoa and Chocolate Industry in the 19th Century
Rowntree BS	1941	Poverty and Progress
Rowntree BS	1951	Poverty and the Welfare State
Vagner, G.	1989	The Chocolate Conscience
Vernon, A.		A Quaker Business Man
Waddilove, L.E.	1954	One Mans Vision The Story of the Joseph Rowntree Village Trust
Worstenholme	1986	Joseph Rowntree 1836–1925